THE FIRST AND ONLY BOOK OF

36 Years of Cartoons for the Star Tribune

BY STEVE SACK

★ StarTribune

The First and Only Book of Sack: 36 Years of Cartoons for the Star Tribune

Cartoons and text: Steve Sack
Editor: David Banks
Designer: Mike Rice
Author photo: Jeff Wheeler

For information about permission to reproduce selections from this book, write to
John Wareham, Star Tribune, 650 3rd Ave. South, Suite 1300, Minneapolis, Minnesota, 55488.

ISBN: 978-0-692-90838-9

First U.S. edition 2017

For Beth,
for making me laugh every day.

Richard M. Nixon by
U.S. Sen. Al Franken

FOREWORD

Written and compiled by David Banks,
assistant commentary editor, Star Tribune

Like most people, I try to live a humble life, one that does useful things in the world and limits any detrimental impact on other people and the planet. But, inevitably, I produce some garbage. So, once a week, a large truck ambles down my street — diesel engine rumbling, brake system hissing — usually before I am ready to open my eyes. It is an awakening.

And not necessarily a welcome one. But then I remember that the sanitation workers are there to take stock of my mess, deal with it, and move on. For the moment, I've been cleansed, given new opportunity.

A daily editorial cartoon serves something like this purpose — think of it as sanitation for a free society. Through caricature, clever setups, and allusions both direct and subtle, it points out the ways in which we, and our leaders, fail to live up to our better instincts, and to the logical inconsistencies we deploy as cover.

Then again, sometimes a cartoon just reminds us to have fun.

Every day there's a blank slate to fill, and since the 1980s at Minnesota's largest newspaper, Steve Sack has been at that drawing board. That's nearly a quarter of the 150-year history the Star Tribune is celebrating in 2017.

As the paper's assistant commentary editor during some of Steve's tenure, I can confidently say he's one of the best in the business. But don't just take my word for it. Take it from those who've been on the receiving end of his wit:

I used to do political cartoons myself in high school. I did a pretty good Nixon. But I couldn't draw in three dimensions, so I gave up. Steve Sack, though, has a drawing style that is uniquely his own. I must say that I wasn't terribly happy with his caricature of me, until one morning when I had just finished shaving and, looking in the mirror, thought to myself, "I look like a Sack cartoon of me."

And if you look at any collection of his work, you'll understand Steve's breadth as a journalist and his skill as a commentator. I've seen him fearlessly skewer the arrogant, the evil, and the incompetent with surgical precision. I've also seen him aim his pen to lift up heroes, and to help people see things in a new light.

As someone who has often used the written and spoken word to call out absurdity, hypocrisy, and lies, I've always marveled at the ability of a skilled editorial cartoonist like Steve to do the same with pictures. He has that rare ability to capture exactly what we all should be thinking about the issues of the day, if only we were as smart — or as clever — as he is.

When he won the Pulitzer Prize in Editorial Cartooning 2013, I wasn't surprised. Nobody in Minnesota was. We'd seen his work on the Star Tribune editorial page for so long that we were spoiled by the regularity of his talent. The only surprise was that he hadn't won one earlier.

Steve Sack is a master of his craft, and his longtime impact on our local, state, and national dialogue is unquestioned. I hope this collection of his work will help everyone understand what a gem we've had for so long tucked within the Op-Ed pages of our state's largest newspaper.

U.S. Sen. Al Franken

The job of the editorial cartoonist may be one of the most difficult in any newspaper. In an age of 140-character tweets and 10-second Snapchats, Steve Sack makes you think, weaving the news of the day into drawings that speak far more than a thousand words. He has poked fun at the most powerful in American life with a deft understanding of his job as an editorial cartoonist. (That job isn't to make powerful people seem funny. It is to remind them, and his readers, that they are only human. Humans who sometimes do silly, stupid, outrageous, and inspiring things in public life.) We live in a society where the mediums for communicating opinions and ideas have never been broader or more ubiquitous. Yet, Steve has elevated his art and craft to such a level that he has transitioned into an era in which his work has never been more necessary or more relevant.

Steve doesn't approach his work with an eye toward making fun of how someone looks. That's not what captures his attention. It's how they act and behave that moves his creative mind onto the pages of the newspaper. I've been the target of Steve's biting editorial commentary. I'd be lying if I didn't tell you that I found a certain sense of foreboding in seeing his representation of Norm Coleman in the newspaper. There's a tremendous sense of humility that one in public life finds after seeing themselves through the Steve's eyes and art. After the gulp in my throat subsided, I had a good chuckle.

Today, American politics needs more humor, and more of our politicians need to get a sense of humor. Thankfully, Steve's work will continue to remind those in public life that they should never take themselves too seriously. Because Steve sure won't.

Former U.S. Sen. Norm Coleman

Or, you could take it from one of his fellow cartoonists:

Among his peers, a disparate group of sometimes jealous and highly competitive people, Steve Sack is uniformly beloved and respected. I do not say this lightly. He's one of the few cartoonists all agree is so broadly talented and innovative that we just collectively stand back and think, "Wow. I wish I could do that/ think of that/draw like that." Not only that, he's just, well, so personally nice. He makes nice people in Minnesota look like uncivilized louts from, say, Wisconsin. His work, however, is often not nice at all: it's brutal, artistically brilliant, and thoughtful. The Star Tribune is fortunate to have him commenting there, and our profession is proud to be his colleague. If they can think of a prize higher than the Pulitzer, he should get that, too. He is also shy, and it would embarrass him. But he deserves it.

Jack Ohman, Sacramento Bee
(Winner of the 2016 Pulitzer Prize in Editorial Cartooning)

But, most important, take it from his audience:

To his followers, Steve Sack demonstrates again and again that there is no shortage of imaginative metaphors in the upstairs warehouse. In one of his magical offerings, he called up the skills of the visual artist, the writer, the comedian, and the political commentator. All were necessary, as Steve had selected an astounding visual metaphor that he alone could execute: the divided sentiments of the entire nation in a bottle! (Technically, it was an undulating, glowing lava lamp.) That hilarious cartoon masterpiece debuted on Father's Day of 2016, and you'll find it reproduced in this book. Steve was spot-on, illuminating our enchantment with raw personality and our distress over national politics.

Steve's career has never lacked for praise and awards. But the highest accolades are reserved for those who can delight a classroom, an audience, or a readership in order to transfer knowledge — in short, to teach. Steve is that entertaining professor, directing us into the often-difficult lessons of cultural identity.

There may be a bias to Steve's work, but it is tilted toward artistry and human dignity. His focus is on techniques that will elevate a unique metaphor and its underlying critical message. Which raises the question: Is there a better word for his creations than "cartoons"?

Just one more way to acknowledge these high achievements: Continue the honorarium we call a newspaper subscription. That would be an ongoing salute to Steve Sack and his long-standing art patron and publisher, the Star Tribune. After all, it was the Star Trib who let the cartoon genie out of the bottle in 1981, granting him freedom to fly.

Steve Watson, Minneapolis, subscriber since the 1970s

Over several months in early 2017, Steve Sack and I reviewed the several thousand cartoons he's made over the years. The collection that follows is not necessarily meant to be a comprehensive history of events, although it touches on many major moments and personalities. Nor is it an exhaustive review of Steve's work. (He'd be the first to tell you that he produced some of his own garbage.) But it includes some of the best, including cartoons for which he was awarded the Pulitzer in 2013 and was a finalist three other times — in 2004, 2016 and 2017.

In my work at the paper, I read most of the letters to the editor. It's not infrequent to encounter one that goes like this: *Does Steve Sack have a book of his cartoons? If not, he should.*

Right you are. Here you go.

DJB

INTRODUCTION

Imagine you had the opportunity to see the total results of your work — every day's effort for your entire career. For teachers, that would be every class taught, every parent/teacher meeting, every wild and swinging MEA convention. For a cop, every speeding ticket, every crime solved, every doughnut-fueled stakeout. Or for a proctologist — well, you get the picture.

I just went over my "every day's" work for the past 36 years at the Star Tribune. Don't check my math, but that's more than 8,000 drawings. I create a cartoon five days a week to fill my bit of real estate on our opinion pages, whether inspired or not.

I found it interesting how well I remember drawing most of them. Each had my entire attention for a day, beginning as a gleam in my eye, through sometimes agonizing birth pains, and eventually being sent out into the world. They are all my children, my babies — even the ones I'd like to lock away from unforgiving public eyes.

I've characterized my job description as "read the paper, crack a joke, draw a picture, and turn it in." My "beat" is quite simply everything in the universe — the serious, the sad, the interesting, the just plain wacky. In short, I cartoon on everything people are talking about.

The following are some of my efforts. Not all of them, because, frankly, many were just not that good: overly long captions, outdated analogies, forgotten faces. Some I couldn't find due to corrupted computer files. And then there's the landfill laughably referred to as my filing system.

Here's how we organized the book: first, our presidents, from Ronald Reagan to Donald Trump. Then, national and international topics, and finally, my local-issue cartoons. I didn't think a simple chronological order made sense, because that would sandwich, say, a silly pothole cartoon between two cartoons on the horrors of war or rampaging disease.

A few thank-yous: to the late Charles Bailey of the Minneapolis Tribune for hiring me way back when. To my editor, Scott Gillespie, and to all of the talented editorial writers, reporters, photographers and assorted staff of the Star Tribune for support and friendship. And to this book's editor, David Banks, and designer, Mike Rice, for their incredible effort slapping this thing together.

Steve Sack
May 2017

2/26/82

Minneapolis Tribune

4/19/81

Ronald Reagan

The cartoon on this page was one of my first for the Minneapolis Tribune. President Reagan was a strong supporter of gun rights both before and after the attempt on his life in 1981. His severely injured press secretary, James Brady, went on to become a strong advocate for sensible gun legislation.

When I speak to groups, the cartoon on the facing page is the first I show. As a kid, I thought one day I'd become an artist for an advertising agency. To that end, I took business classes in college, looking toward a degree in marketing. Unfortunately, I flunked Accounting 101 — three times. So instead I work for a major newspaper dispensing economic advice to the president of the United States. Is this a great country or what?

11/22/85

Reagan's military buildup and aggressive foreign policy also featured bold peace initiatives with the Soviets.

7/29/83

While his administration had its share of economic failures and scandals, Reagan coasted along on his easy charm.

RE-READ MY LIPS

NO **MORE** NEW TAXES AND THIS TIME I REALLY REALLY MEAN IT UNLESS OF COURSE THE DEMOCRATS FORCE ME BUT BOY, OH, BOY I'LL FIGHT IT BECAUSE I **REALLY** BELIEVE WATCH THIS SPACE

SACK
STAR TRIBUNE

11/4/92

3/8/92

7/31/92

George H.W. Bush

Bush's re-election campaign was hampered by a lousy economy. Having chosen the hilariously lightweight Dan Quayle as his vice president didn't help.

11/4/92

Bill Clinton

After 12 years of Republican rule, America was hungry for something new ...

... but Bill Clinton's presidency was marred by an entirely different appetite.

1/21/98

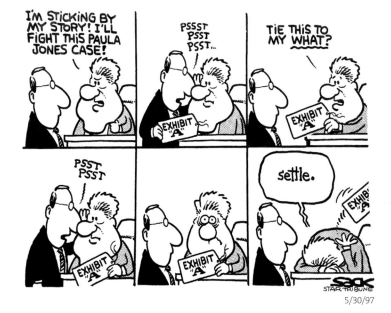

5/30/97

I didn't think Clinton should be impeached over the Monica Lewinsky affair. To me the appropriate punishment was a lifetime of ridicule from every comedian, late-night host, and editorial cartoonist in the country. I've done my bit!

In spite of failures in health care and a string of assorted scandals, Clinton left office with no major wars and a national budget surplus.

12/30/96

1/26/96

2/18/01

1/26/96

11/9/00

George W. Bush

The George W. Bush-Al Gore presidential election of 2000 was a squeaker, with a recount process that lasted more than a month. Eventually, the Supreme Court intervened, giving the win to Bush (who, um, didn't really get the most votes).

7/2/03

1/9/03

6/8/06

The "compassionate conservative" showed particular compassion for those who needed it least.

Scientists began raising alarm about a new threat — global warming. With a big wet kiss to special interests, science denial became conservative orthodoxy.

10/1/94

3/1/04

SOUL-GAZING WITH PUTIN...

STAR TRIBUNE
SACK

OPPRESSION

2/28/05

Bush said he looked into Vladimir Putin's eyes and could get a sense of the Russian leader's soul. Without a microscope?

9/26/01

9/11/01

9/11

I wasn't satisfied with this cartoon. Sept. 11, 2001, was a chaotic day, one every American adult vividly remembers. I got the first reports from home. When I arrived downtown, the newsroom was abuzz, televisions blaring everywhere. The plan was to release a special edition. I had only a few hours to come up with a cartoon. We still didn't know who exactly was responsible or if more was to come. I drew the simple depiction you see here, inspired by the classic cartoon that Bill Mauldin had created upon the assassination of President John Kennedy (a statue of Lincoln with head in hands). Most of my fellow cartoonists took similar approaches — tearful Statues of Liberty, weeping eagles. I've thought back many times about what I could have drawn to more uniquely express our collective grief.

Opposite page: There were many heroes that day — police, firefighters, first responders — and uncounted acts of courage by ordinary citizens.

CAREFUL, CAREFUL....

CIVIL LIBERTIES

WAR ON TERROR

Sack
STAR TRIBUNE

9/20/01

The entire country was upended. The questionable Patriot Act was intended to protect us. Above all, Americans wanted the perpetrators brought to justice.

STAR TRIBUNE
Sack

YOU CAN RUN TO THE END OF THE EARTH...

THROUGH THE FARTHEST VALLEY...

BEHIND THE LARGEST ROCK...

INTO THE DEEPEST HOLE...

AND BURROW AS FAR AS YOU CAN.

FREEZE.

—BUT WE'LL STILL FIND YOU.

9/16/01

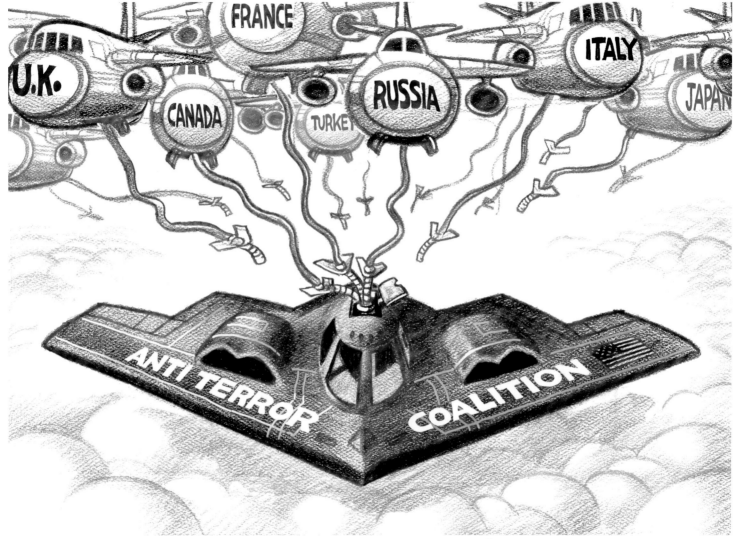

MIDFLIGHT REFUELING

10/4/01

Bush deftly assembled an international coalition to confront the terrorists in their sanctuary of Afghanistan.
No one expected that the operation would become a decadeslong exercise in nation-building.

THE NIGHTMARE

WMD

Sack
STAR TRIBUNE

4/4/03

Iraq

I fell for it, too. When Gen. Colin Powell, as secretary of state, spoke before the United Nations Security Council and declared proof of weapons of mass destruction in Iraq, I believed him.

"HIGH NOON"

1/19/03

Even though the war in Afghanistan was still raging, Bush picked his next target. Iraqi President Saddam Hussein blustered as the United Nations sent inspectors to find his weapons of mass destruction. But this time Bush's "coalition of the willing" wasn't.

"NO DECISION HAS BEEN MADE..."

10/4/03

As U.N. weapons inspectors scoured Iraq for evidence of WMDs, the Bush administration relentlessly made its preparations.

STAR TRIBUNE
SACK

4/10/03

The Iraqi Army was no match for American military might.

Days turned to months, and months turned to years. Where were the WMDs?

9/23/04

Bush wanted to assure a nervous public that everything was under control.

'WE'RE READY TO BEGIN PRE-BOARDING...'

2/23/04

Iraq had to be rebuilt from the ground up. Vice President Dick Cheney had the same answer for any problem.

9/2/02

Bush's fear-based re-election campaign boiled down to one simple message: Vote for me or the terrorists win!

3/26/03

The grim toll mounted: 1,000 soldiers lost, 2,000, 3,000 ...

7/27/03

5/20/04

3/6/02

It became painfully evident that the military approach was making things worse. Problems flared across the globe.

8/24/03

Bush donned a flight suit and landed
on an aircraft carrier to celebrate
"Mission Accomplished."
He came to rue that phrase.

5/4/03

In a shameful policy of desperation, the Bush administration approved the use of torture on prisoners of war. The horror stories mounted: Abu Ghraib, Guantanamo, black sites, rendition ...

THE SLIPPERY SLOPE

5/24/04

6/24/04

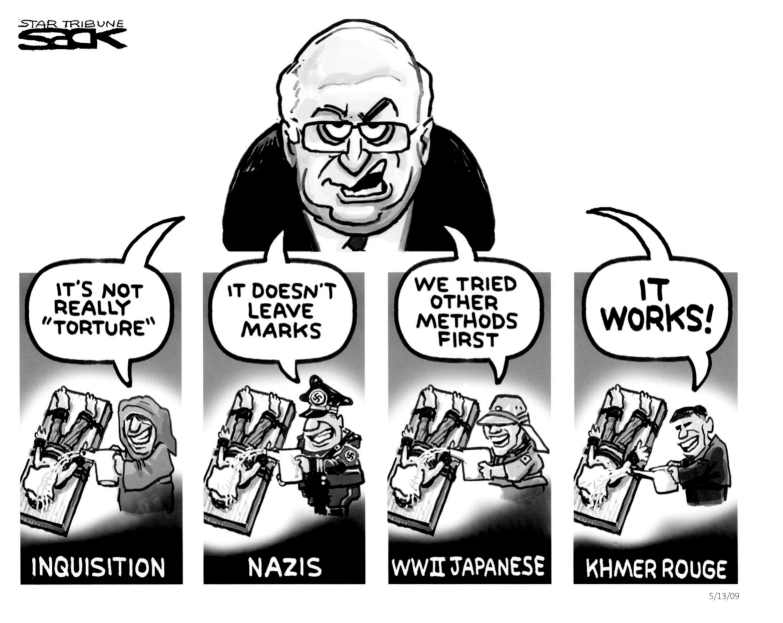

5/13/09

Cheney gave his torture regime the blandly Orwellian title "enhanced interrogation."

10/29/07

The Geneva Conventions, meant
to uphold humanity during wartime,
were an impediment to the
administration's strategy.
The world took note.

9/20/06

The grim tide of war.

Years of nonstop warfare pushed our troops to the breaking point.

Tours in Afghanistan and Iraq were extended beyond their usual lengths, and many in the military returned to those battle zones several times.

8/24/06

4/16/07

11/17/06

'THE MORE DIVIDED WE BECOME, THE MORE WE ALL END UP TOGETHER.'

9/11/06

For all the spin about imminent success, the public wasn't buying it. Congress was slow to hold the Bush administration accountable.

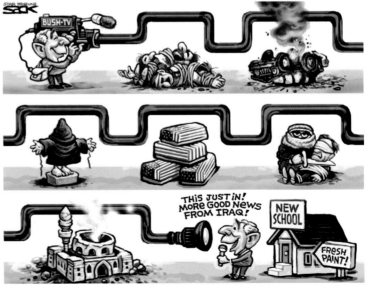

4/21/06

Everyone knows the phrase: If you're in a hole, stop digging. Well, almost everyone ...

THE PLAN

9/10/07

A last-ditch "surge" policy had some success, at least enough to get through the end of Bush's second term.

'FOR MY NEXT NUMBER....'

So many evildoers, so little time ...

10/12/09

The United States isn't the first country to have spent years and lives on Afghanistan, just the latest.

1/22/07

— 'AND IN THIS CORNER ....'

1/26/07

12/14/06

Democrats were lining up to retake the White House. After a tough primary season, Barack Obama prevailed over Hillary Clinton with a message of "hope and change." He easily defeated Republican John McCain in the general election.

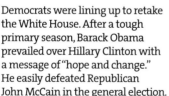

IT'S MY 154-POINT PLAN TO REFUTE THE CHARGE THAT I'M TOO CALCULATING.

12/19/07

Bump.

Barack Obama

Regardless of their vote, most Americans took pride in the fact that, 145 years after Abraham Lincoln's Emancipation Proclamation, the nation had elected its first African-American president.

1/12/09

The instant-classic Obama victory headline from satirical newspaper The Onion: "Black Man Given Nation's Worst Job."

My all-time most popular cartoon — among conservatives. I've seen this one reprinted on more right-wing blogs, websites, and Facebook posts than I can count.

2/3/10

2/16/09

Obama's early years as president were consumed with digging us out of the worst recession since the Great Depression.

Gaffe-meister Joe Biden offered comic relief.

10/24/08

8/21/09

Despite total Republican opposition, Obama's massive health care reform became the law of the land. You'd think he'd have put more effort into the rollout.

10/23/14

Surprise, surprise. Despite Obama's decisive re-election in 2012, he was met with monolithic resistance by the new Republican Congress.

Republicans had their own sources of information on the issue of climate change. Usually in the form of fossil-fuel-industry lobbyists.

Winding down wars isn't as easy as it sounds.

Some fires just won't go out.

9/5/13

Nobel Peace Prize winner Barack Obama expanded bombing to seven countries, authorizing 10 times more drone strikes than had George W. Bush.

3/26/14

2/7/15

The U.S. trade embargo on Cuba is an outdated, failed policy. Obama sought to turn that around, becoming the first U.S. president to visit Cuba since 1928. Viva Obama!

5/9/13

3/30/11

The tragic attack on America's consulate in Benghazi, Libya, deserved a thorough investigation. But seven congressional probes over two years? A few Republicans admitted that the goal was primarily to inflict damage on presidential candidate Hillary Clinton.

5/5/14

ECLiPSeS

9/13/15

6/30/16

4/17/16

2/12/16

The 2016 campaign

Hillary Clinton had been the presumed front-runner for the 2016 Democratic Party nomination since Obama's first day in office. Imagine her surprise to hear footsteps from a 74-year-old "democratic socialist" from Vermont.

Opposite page: Of course, Clinton had been the presumed front-runner for the 2008 Democratic nomination as well. That time, she was upstaged by the 47-year-old junior senator from Illinois.

2/27/16

Both the policy proposals and
campaign strategy of Bernie Sanders
were hampered by wishful thinking.
In the end, he got 1,894 of the
2,382 delegates needed to win the
Democratic nomination.

5/4/16

2016

5/31/15

There was no shortage of volunteers on the GOP side to repeal and replace President Obama.
The party's 17 candidates made for some crowded debate stages.

The Republican establishment's favorite candidate, Jeb Bush, was hampered by the memory of his older brother's failures.

One by one, the candidates fell to the irresistible momentum of ...

Donald Trump

It's very important to get the name right, because it's everywhere — on buildings, on planes, on casinos, on golf courses, even on slabs of meat. And in 2016, on your election ballot!

8/9/15

With the media's unwitting assistance, the primary season became a crazy sideshow with the most implausible, unconventional star.

Naturally, he was endorsed by a previous election campaign's most implausible, unconventional star, Sarah Palin.

1/23/16

Trump broke every rule in the book. No comment was too vulgar, no position too outlandish, no cheap schoolyard attack too undignified.

Every presidential candidate in the modern age disclosed income tax information. Except Mr. Trump. One wonders why.

9/11/16

Trump's odd admiration for the murderous Russian leader Vladimir Putin upended decades of Republican orthodoxy. For anyone else, it would have been disqualifying.

U.S. ELECTION

PUTIE

ASSANGE

HACKERSACK

Julian Assange of WikiLeaks was the guy who helped Putin help Trump. Carefully timed e-mail leaks kept Clinton's campaign reeling.

8/3/16

Was I wrong about this one! Instead of leading down-ballot Republicans to their doom, Trump would usher in a wave of GOP wins across the country. That said, Khizr Khan was right: For his country, Trump sacrificed NOTHING.

10/16/16

Last-minute surprise: The Billy Bush "Access Hollywood" grab-'em-by-the-you-know-whats tape is released.
Trump's shameless vulgarity was laid bare in a scandal from which no candidate for America's highest office could recover. Right?

Election night

Uncertainty is a pain. Some cartoonists get around this by drawing a cartoon for either outcome. In our last presidential election, the polls were tight enough that I actually drew three cartoons — one to be published in the event of a Hillary Clinton victory, one for a Donald Trump win, and one for "no decision at presstime."

We used the "no-decision" cartoon in the early edition before going to "Trump wins." And, no, they didn't pay me extra for doing triple my usual work.

I hope to God this happened.

11/25/16

Trump not only presented us with a bewildering array of conflicts of interest, he showed little interest in mitigating them.

MY ADMINISTRATION (CLUNK, BOING) IS LIKE A (THUD, SNAP) FINE-TUNED MACHINE! (THUNKA-THUNKA DING DONG)

2/19/17

KEEP CALM AND ...WAIT— GOOD LORD! DID YOU SEE WHAT HE'S DOING NOW???

1/25/17

What with the ridiculous tweets, awful Cabinet appointments, and unsettling first contacts with our allies, every day seemed crazier than the last.

WHEN WORLD LEADERS HEAR THAT PRESIDENT TRUMP IS ON THE LINE....

PUTIN

2/4/17

11/19/16

Trump's oft-repeated campaign promise to "drain the Washington swamp" was the first of many to be blithely tossed aside.

12/1/16

1/22/17

Compulsive Tweeter-in-Chief Trump could not control himself. Even his die-hard supporters wished he'd give it a rest already.

1/14/17

THE HATE WHISPERER

BANNON

11/16/16

With the naming of Steve Bannon as political strategist, the change in tone for the nation's highest office could not have been more stark.

1/20/17

1/24/17

Trump's horrifying "American carnage" inaugural address was answered the very next day:
The Women's March on Washington was the largest demonstration in our capital's history.

THE LiFe OF A WHiTE HOUSe SPOKeSPeRSON

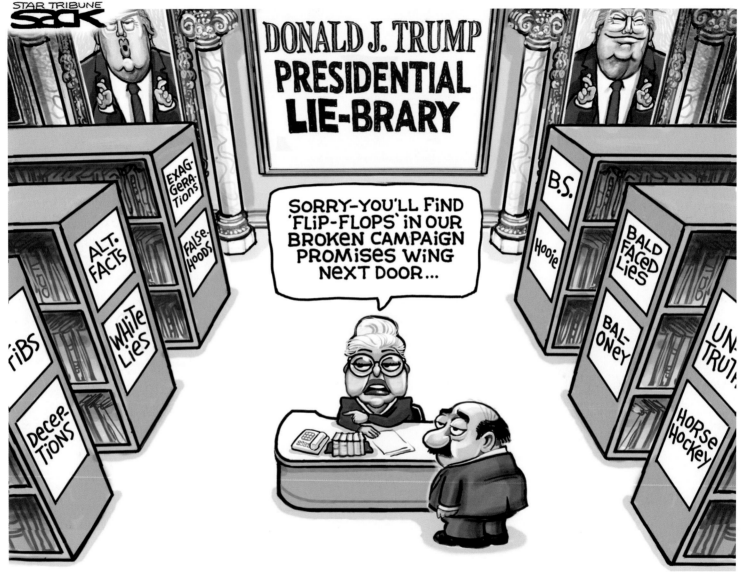

Fact-checkers documented nearly 500 false or misleading claims by President Trump about subjects big and small in his first 100 days. For him, it's like breathing.

Top cop FBI chief James Comey was investigating Russia's involvement in the election. Trump canned him.

5/11/17

Responding to aggressive missile tests, Trump threatened North Korea with his mighty armada. If only he had a clue where it was.

4/27/17

3/1/17

The Trump government was taking shape. And what a shape it was.

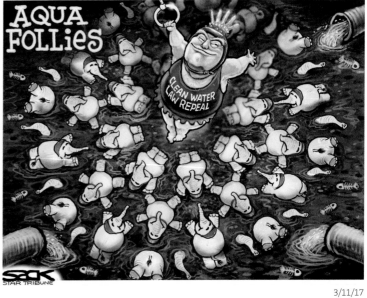

3/11/17

4/6/17

5/13/17

We thought the Trumpcare bill that Republicans slapped together was the worst possible ...

... and then we saw their second version.

5/5/17

STAR TRIBUNE
sack

FiRST
FoReiGN
TRiP

UNITED S

5/21/17

So here we are. As of this writing, Donald Trump was four months into his presidency. A special counsel was on his trail over the Russia business. Would Trump face impeachment? Would he "Make America Great Again" or turn the planet into a burning dystopia? Stay tooned!

THE WORK OF A CARTOONIST

Occasionally, I'm invited to speaking engagements. Following are answers to some of the questions I frequently receive about my job that aren't addressed elsewhere in this book.

How it all began

I started editorial cartooning at the University of Minnesota in 1976. I had joined the student newspaper, the Daily, as a part-time illustrator. I was making between 15 and 40 bucks a night creating illustrations to go along with feature stories and movie reviews. It was a wonderful place to start — they had about five artists. They also had a staff cartoonist, who I noted was being paid more than the illustrators. When he took a leave of absence, I hopped into his chair and was immediately enchanted by the Glamorous Cartoonist Lifestyle.

The joy of drawing

Almost all kindergartners love to draw. It's the few who don't stop who go on to become visual creatives. The subjects I most liked to draw then are my favorites still: dinosaurs, space aliens, wacky machines, monsters. I doodle incessantly, anywhere and everywhere. Is it possible to survive a staff meeting without scribbling flying saucers or monsters devouring Donald Trump? I don't want to find out.

On style

For most of my career, I've felt unsure about my artwork. Starting out, I was very much influenced by artists I admired, as is true of most young artists. There is no real school or arts program specific to this art form, so basically you learn from what you see. The giants of my industry at the time were Pat Oliphant, Jeff MacNelly, and Mike Peters. They represented a new wave of cartooning that began in the 1960s with Oliphant moving from Australia to the Denver Post. Pat brought a rollicking irreverence to a field that had been dominated since its inception by a more serious approach best exemplified by Herblock and Bill Mauldin. Oliphant's work inspired both MacNelly and Peters and virtually every cartoonist since. Add to that influence a heavy dose of Mad magazine and Warner Bros. animated cartoons, and you'll see the formative roots of most of today's American political cartoonists.

As a beginner, I wanted to both draw exactly like and entirely different from my cartoon heroes. I experimented with materials a lot (inspired by another fearlessly experimenting cartoon hero, the great Dwane Powell): ink and pen, watercolor, charcoal, colored pencil, Sharpie marker, technical pens, digital tablet, and, most lately, an iPad. I even tried playing with 3-D computer imaging, but the results were too visually distracting. Ultimately, I am comfortable with the Quest for the Perfect Style being an unachievable goal. Most great cartoonists and other artists have made stylistic changes to their work over the course of their careers. Clearly they were in a constant search for a better way to express their ideas. For that reason, I've become more comfortable with just doing my best and always being hungry to improve.

On caricature

Caricature is tricky. The goal is not so much to simply exaggerate a subject's most prominent features but to find a deeper truth about the person. Editorial cartoon caricatures are best when they instantly identify the person and seemlessly integrate them in the scene or premise of the cartoon. While you want to make the image as funny (or horrific) as possible, overdoing the caricature exaggeration could distract from the message.

I've always felt that an appealing style is an essential component of a cartoon. However harsh a situation is being addressed, or how vile and disgusting a particular world figure may be, it is more effective to create nicely designed imagery to convey the cartoon's ultimate message. True, some characters are so horrible that the temptation is to draw them as ugly as possible to match their deeds. But that tips off the viewer before they even get to understand the message being conveyed. One cartoonist regularly drew George W. Bush with fangs and a banana republic dictator's uniform, regardless of the content of the cartoon. I imagine a lot of readers wouldn't bother to read further once the message was so crudely telegraphed. So when I draw a politician's face, I try to have fun with his or her features without crossing into meanness for meanness' sake. Yes, that's a matter of taste. I'm sure I've crossed that line many times in some readers' eyes.

The power of cuteness

The comedian Conan O'Brien had a terrific bit on this subject. He suggested that cuteness is the most powerful force in the world, more powerful than any evil, and set up a demonstration to prove it. He presented to his audience a box full of kittens and puppies. The tiny creatures were all dressed in Nazi uniforms and Ku Klux Klan robes. They were still adorable! This told me that a concept can have a pleasant (even sweet) appearance that on further examination could examine darker truths. The great cartoonists of macabre humor, such as Charles Addams, Gahan Wilson, and B. Kliban, used enormously appealing artwork to draw you into their dark and twisted worldviews.

On reader reaction

Generally, it's true that when a reader really likes a cartoon they'll put it on their refrigerator or cubicle wall. If they hate it, they let me know by email, letter, or phone. Or they let my boss know. Or my boss' boss.

That said, reader reaction has changed a bit over the years. In the pre-internet Stone Age I got a *lot* of mail. That changed as papers went online. I don't think it was because those readers were coming around to my way of thinking. More likely they had new outlets for expressing their dissent.

Some cartoonists take pride in vicious hate mail, as if that were some measure of "doing your job." I don't see it that way. Ultimately, I think about the advice I got from Charles Bailey, the Minneapolis Tribune executive editor who hired me. He said: "Never hesitate to make people angry with a cartoon, but know *why* they are getting angry." That is so true. I prefer that people like my cartoons, and I'm OK with them disliking or even hating them. The only thing that really bothers me is when they don't "get" the cartoon. That indicates failure on my part to be clear in my message.

My all-time favorite hate letter

A few years back, I received a three-page letter about an issue then raging in our state — same-sex marriage. My cartoons had been supportive. The letter writer was not. The letter actually began quite well. He laid out his argument, gave examples, and quoted notables in support of his position. But after two pages of reasonable debate, he let loose with a string of insults. He concluded by saying that he wanted to crumple all of my cartoons and toss them into the gutter, and that he refrained only because he didn't want such foul litter offending his neighbors.

With that, he signed his name. Even included his address. Turns out he lived just down the block.

So I wrote him back a respectful letter, answered his debate points with mine, agreed to disagree, and thanked him for keeping our neighborhood gutters tidy.

This biz

When I started my cartooning career, there were around 300 full-time staff cartoonists in America. Today there are fewer than 50 (plus a few dozen internet, freelancer and part-timers). Back then, there were maybe three to five openings at newspapers per year as cartoonists retired, were fired, or expired. Newcomers at least had a reasonable chance.

As the newspaper industry contracted, fewer and fewer papers had the budget to support a cartoonist. As family-owned papers were sold to chains, there was less inclination to publish material that might ruffle an advertiser's feathers. It's said that one has better odds of becoming a U.S. senator than a newspaper editorial cartoonist.

It's a somewhat lonely gig. Usually, you are the only art person in a sea of word people. I was fortunate to have a fellow cartoonist, my good friend Craig Macintosh, on staff with me for a number of years at the Star Tribune. It was great to share with a fellow pro about struggles with art or ideas. Eventually, though, Craig moved on, and now focuses on his new career as a thriller novelist.

So, for the most part, editorial cartoonists are scattered across the country. We have an organization called the AAEC — American Association of Editorial Cartoonists — that advocates on issues and difficulties concerning our unique craft. We hold an annual convention in various cities that includes panel discussions, presentations by noted artists, and, occasionally, speeches by public figures. But the most important aspect of those gatherings is social, revisiting friends we see in person generally once a year, as well as meeting and encouraging those coming up the ranks. With the internet, it's now easier to stay connected. But nothing beats being able to zing a buddy in person with a drawing scrawled on a cocktail napkin in a seedy bar somewhere far from home.

There was one time our group was invited to a talk in the White House Rose Garden by Ronald Reagan. He was most gracious to a group that didn't always treat him the same. The event was marred slightly after the talk when a member of our group unexpectedly rushed the president's podium. He only wanted Reagan's autograph in a book he had brought. As the president kindly signed the book, I looked up and saw sharpshooters on the roof surveying the scene. The Secret Service later informed us that the cartoonist had come within seconds of being "neutralized." One can only imagine the cartoons we would have drawn about *that*.

On the power of cartoons

Are my editorial cartoons effective? I used to answer that question by saying I elected Barack Obama twice and drove Congresswoman Michele Bachmann from office. Then came the victory of Donald Trump, and I will happily plead impotence and let my conservative colleagues assume responsibility for that monstrosity.

Truth be told, I don't think editorial cartoons today have much real power to effect change or sway opinion. At most, they rally those already on the cartoonist's side. I've probably seen more cartoons than most readers of this book, and I can't recall one that changed my mind about an issue. More likely, they presented an argument I hadn't considered, or framed an issue with useful clarity, or brought some cause attention it deserves.

In the days of our great cartooning forefather Thomas Nast, cartoonists were indeed influential. Heck, Mr. Nast famously brought down the corrupt politician Boss Tweed of Tammany Hall, whatever *that* was. When you're not competing with radio or television or movies or the internet, it is a bit easier getting the public's undivided attention.

7/24/06

Spiraling gas prices had a massive effect on both our economy and foreign policy. They can't invent those solar-powered flying cars soon enough!

7/9/06

Ninety-seven percent of all the climate scientists in the world believe global warming is real. I'm not smarter than a climate scientist. Are you?

4/14/16

SiGNS of the TiMes

4/8/07

12/17/07

12/4/16

8/31/03

5/10/17

The Environmental Protection Agency
has a spotty enforcement record.
Under Trump, it's likely to get spottier.
(But I like that environment cartoons
give me a chance to draw critters.)

3/30/17

9/4/00

8/3/95

6/23/08

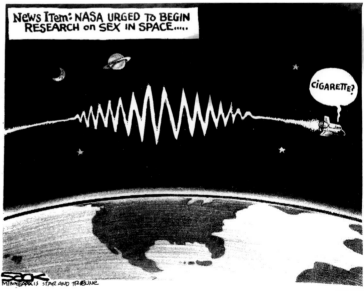

7/1/85

9/30/12

2/9/15

Farmers live at the mercy of the weather — and Washington.

4/5/07

8/26/99

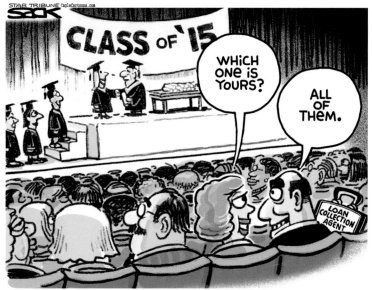

5/17/15

5/21/03

6/4/15

'IT WAS BAD ENOUGH WHEN THEY STARTED CHARGING FOR IN-FLIGHT MEALS...'

1/13/03

1/8/10

The French banned "burkinis." Only the French would outlaw bathing suits for showing too little.

I love "cliché" cartoons, meaning those with a setup that's been used a million times, but with a unique twist. Think "man on a desert island" — escaping that Carnival Cruise From Hell. No food, no power, and overflowing toilets.

9/4/16

2/14/13

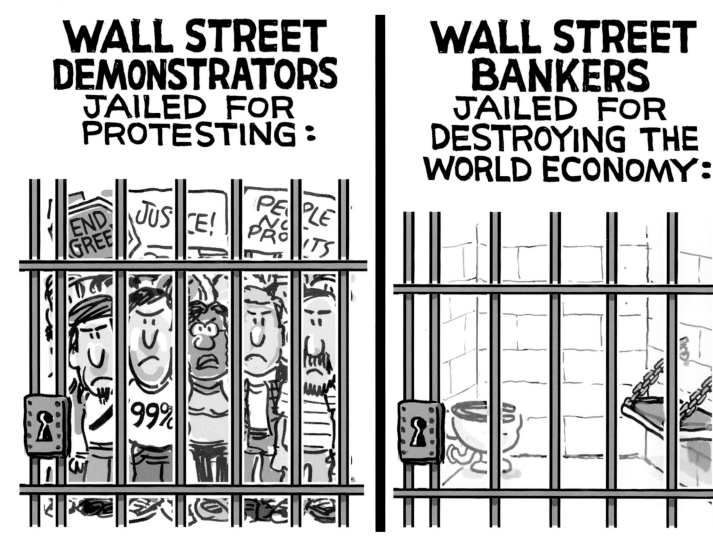

4/6/06

"If all the economists were laid end to end, they would not reach a conclusion." — Attributed to George Bernard Shaw

10/14/04

1/24/10

WHAT iT SEEMS LiKE

6/29/03

The World Wide Wild West.
That spam cartoon was drawn before
hacking was a thing.

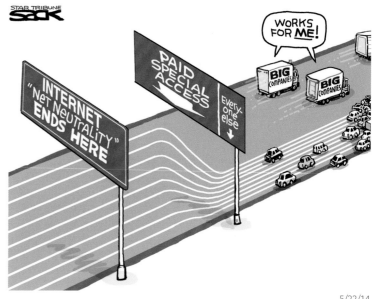

5/22/14

3/26/06

2/4/13

Bird flu, the Zika virus, AIDS, measles — you name the pandemic, and I've cartooned it.

6/17/16

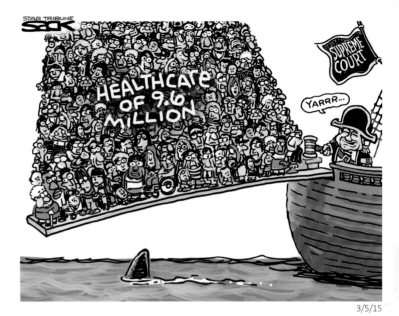

3/5/15

Why is ours the only developed country unwilling to take care of all of its citizens?

3/25/12

LET FREEDOM RING!

5/15/13

MINNESOTA IS CONSIDERING A MARRIAGE AMENDMENT.

YOU LIVE IN IOWA. TELL ME, EXACTLY HOW HAS LEGALIZING GAY MARRIAGE IMPACTED YOURS?

IT'S HORRIBLE. WE USED TO BE A COUPLE UNITED IN MARRIAGE. NOW WE'RE A COUPLE UNITED IN MARRIAGE, BUT SO ARE THE TWO LADIES NEXT DOOR!

EXCEPT THEY REMEMBER EACH OTHER'S ANNIVERSARY... IT'S BEEN A NIGHTMARE!

5/8/11

5/19/04

Massachusetts led the way toward marriage equality back in 2004. It took too many years for the nation to catch up. Minnesota was the first state to achieve marriage equality by popular vote.

Opposite: Now we get into stupid arguments about nonissues like bathroom laws.

9/16/04

America's foolish gun culture accounts for around 30,000 deaths a year on average.
That's more than 1,080,000 Americans killed over the 36 years that I've drawn cartoons on this issue.

1/10/13

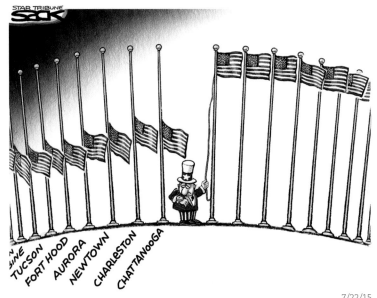

7/22/15

5/20/99

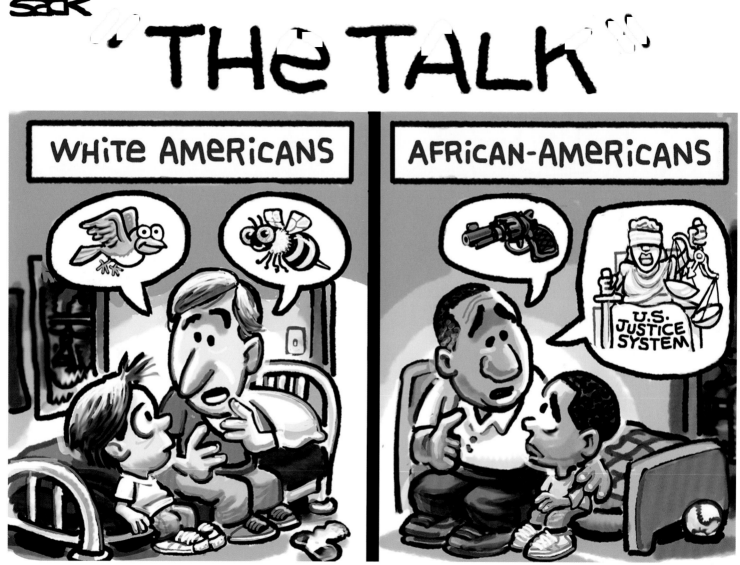

THE TALK

Navigating childhood is not the same for all Americans.

7/17/13

11/9/06

Whoever said it's not whether you win or lose that counts probably lost.

These days, my side usually loses.

11/3/10

LESTER PLUMSQUAT, THE LAST UNDECIDED VOTER IN AMERICA, MISSES THE
ELECTION ENTIRELY WHEN HE'S FACED WITH YET <u>ANOTHER</u> VEXING DECISION...

11/2/04

Gerrymandering, voter ID, cutting back voting hours, reduced polling places — vote-suppression efforts against the nonexistent problem of "vote fraud" are as insidious as they are immoral.

'NOW MAKE HIM RUB HIS TUMMY AND PAT HIS HEAD!'...

7/1/12

STAR TRIBUNE
SACK

CONGRESS

NEUTRAL NEUTRAL
NEUTRAL
NEUTRAL NEUTRAL
NEUTRAL
NEUTRAL VACATION

8/8/13

That some of our lawmakers' actions may be "neutral" is the best we can hope for.

Will Rogers said that we have the best politicians money can buy.

9/27/06

3/29/06

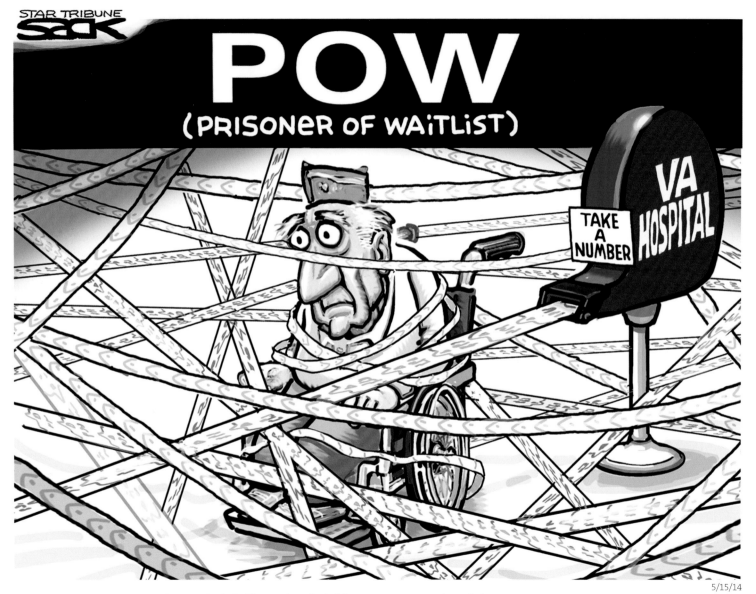

5/15/14

When planning their budgets, politicians don't find hospitals and rehabilitation as sexy as tanks and planes. Our veterans, who give their all, deserve better.

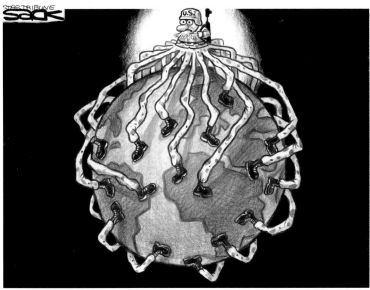

7/14/03

STOWAWAY

12/26/04

1/20/14

Are you feeling more secure?

6/16/13

1/12/03

To paraphrase Dr. Seuss: From here to there, from there to here, scary things are everywhere!

5/4/14

9/22/16

1/7/16

2/17/17

I've drawn many cartoons about
North Korea's deranged leader
Kim Jong Un. And about his daddy
before him. And his daddy's daddy.
The whole crazy Kim clan!

6/23/06

8/16/06

7/10/14

STAR TRIBUNE
Sack

ISIS

GLOBAL SWARMING

9/4/14

1/9/15

Charlie Hebdo

In 2015, two Islamist terrorists attacked the offices of the provocative French satirical magazine Charlie Hebdo. Twelve people were murdered, including four cartoonists. Artists, officials, and ordinary citizens around the world rallied in solidarity for the victims and for the cause of free speech. On visits to cartoon festivals in France, I've met and befriended many French cartoonists (including two of the slain Hebdo artists). It did not surprise me that immediately after the attacks Charlie Hebdo's remaining staff vowed to put out the next edition, on schedule. The usual print run of 60,000 was ultimately raised to 5 million. It sold out immediately. Je suis Charlie.

9/4/14

Our friends from across the pond.

12/8/11

1/13/98

1/13/98

Our Cuba policy is a triumph of
ideology over common sense.

PASSING the BATON

2/22/08

8/21/02

11/20/02

4/7/06

8/15/14

1/25/16

Some personalities are such fun cartoon subjects that we look for any excuse to draw them again.

1/28/14

11/26/03

7/26/13

Bill Cosby, Michael Jackson, and
Anthony Weiner — a gallery of creeps.

12/31/98

10/2/09

8/6/08

4/1/02

On obituary cartoons

I don't especially like drawing these — unless I can find a fresh angle. Summing up a person's life in cartoon form doesn't leave a lot of room for nuance. If it's a good person, you try to depict their signature trait or accomplishment. If it's a bad person, you depict them burning in hell, or deserving to. Often the cartoonist's default is to fall back on the old "St. Peter at the Pearly Gates" shtick. Sometimes simply a nice portrait accompanied by an appropriate quotation says it best.

4/25/95

'NOT WHAT YOU EXPECTED? IF IT'S ANY CONSOLATION — I'M A VIRGIN.'

5/5/11

7/10/06

1/25/89

Above: Disgraced CEO Ken Lay died a few months before his scheduled sentencing in the Enron scandal. The company's bankruptcy cost 20,000 people their jobs and, in many cases, their life savings.

Below: My personal favorite obituary cartoon was for surrealist artist Salvador Dali. I'd like to think that he would have laughed.

Opposite: One of my most popular cartoons was one I thought was overly trite — I commemorated the death of Muppets creator Jim Henson with an image of Kermit the Frog weeping at the base of the "Sesame Street" sign. For years, I've had people show me a wrinkled copy of that cartoon, which for some reason they carried around in their wallet or purse.

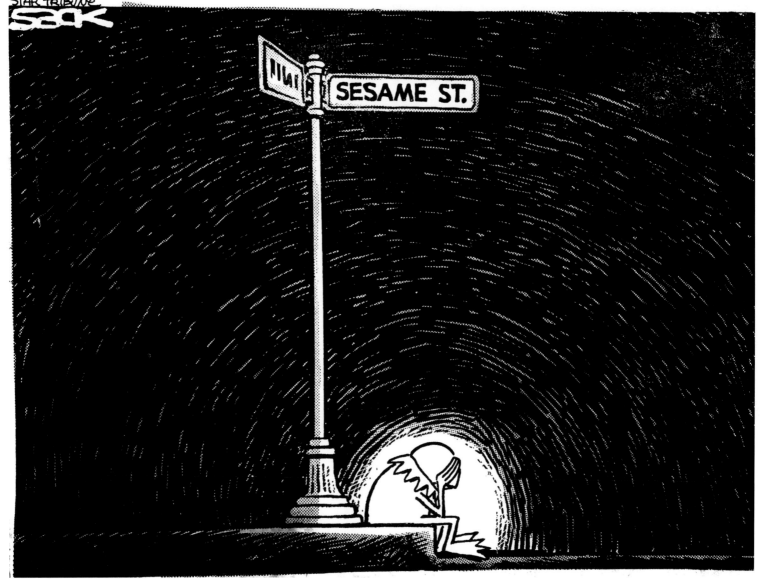

5/18/90

"Politics is what
we create out of
what we do, what
we hope for,
what we dare
to imagine."

Sen. Paul Wellstone
1944-2002

10/26/02

The heartbreak of the Wetterling case touched all of Minnesota.

12/18/85

12/20/06

Some cartoonists look down on weather cartoons, or any cartoon that doesn't have a hard-charging, stand-taking, injustice-eviscerating political or social message. Me? I think anything people are talking about is a good subject for a cartoon. I figure if I can tickle someone's funny bone with a cartoon bemoaning the latest snowstorm or goofy fad, they will come back the next day to see what I'm up to.

The Minnesota first sign of spring.

Sadly, this cartoon could run every year.

Any excuse will do when you're a billionaire wanting a new stadium. I differ with the Star Tribune Editorial Board's philosophy when it comes to publicly funding stadiums.

Like clockwork, every few years some sports scandal or another rolls in.

12/2/11

3/18/99

6/17/03

Caution: Legislature in session!

5/13/15

SWISS
ARNe
KNIFE

5/24/91

4/14/97

1/31/97

Gov. Arne Carlson had a very
particular set of skills.

MY GOVERNOR CAN
BEAT UP MY GOVERNOR.

10/5/99

WORLD'S MOST STRESSFUL JOBS

BUNGEE CORD
LENGTH-TESTER

Hmmm... or was that METRIC?

NITROGLYCERINE BOTTLE
PRICE-STAMPER

THWOMP!
THWOMP!

NITRO
NITR

ELEVATOR MAXIMUM-
CAPACITY ESTIMATOR

SNAP!

GOV. JESSE VENTURA
PRESS SECRETARY

Well, I THINK...

WODELE

10/10/99

MEDIA
PRESS
JACKALS

Thin-skinned Minnesota Gov. Jesse
Ventura had such a contentious
relationship with reporters that he
dubbed them "media jackals."
The State Capitol press corps asked
me to design a T-shirt.

Jesse "the Body" Bigfoot left some big shoes to fill.

5/23/11

Tim "T-paw" Pawlenty had been a typical moderate Republican governor. Then he caught presidential fever.

Unfortunately for him, the ever-colorful Michele Bachmann was eyeing the White House, too.

7/31/11

11/9/12

1/25/07

11/9/11

8/22/11

11/21/82

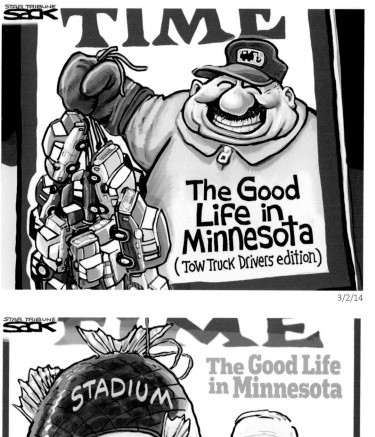

3/2/14

7/15/15

I've re-imagined the iconic Gov. Wendell Anderson's "Good Life" Time magazine cover for every governor, including Rudy Perpich and Mark Dayton, and for other topics as well. At this point, I probably owe them royalties.

7/1/09

I've gotta say I was disappointed that Al Franken had pretty much abandoned his freewheeling sense of humor during his Senate career. But now he has a hilarious new book out. These days we need the funny.

3/11/07

Yes, former U.S. Sen. Norm Coleman was a chameleon; liberal or conservative and everything in between over the years. My favorite persona was his antiwar hippie student leader phase in college.

U.S. Sen. Paul Wellstone wasn't afraid to ruffle feathers.

NO TALKING, NO POINTING, NO STARING, NO PHOTOS, NO PRYING, NO TOUCHING, NO WHISPERS, NO FAWNING, NO AUTOGRAPHS, AND NO EYE CONTACT. WE DON'T WANT TO SCARE HIM AWAY AGAIN, NOW DO WE?....

4/2/92

Garrison Keillor's magnificent creation Lake Wobegon became synonymous with the Minnesota heartland. Mr. Keillor left us for Denmark for two years, but you CAN go home again. Shhhh ... don't scare him off.

It was fun to see him named one of Playgirl's 1986 Sexiest Men Alive. (Also on that year's list: Donald Trump!)

IT'S BEEN A NOT-SO-QUIET WEEK IN LAKE WOBEGON...

8/7/86

ON WINNING THE PULITZER PRIZE

Now that was a strange day!

Most cartoonists enter the Pulitzer competition every year. As with the Oscars or the Super Bowl ring or the State Fair blue ribbon for sheep-shearing, everyone involved has an opinion on who "deserves" to win. I think that, like all such things, it's a combination of skill and luck and your personal gods being in a good mood that day. Plus more luck.

Sometimes the list of winners leaks before the official announcement. The year I was chosen, it came as a complete shock. Instantly, I was herded into the newsroom, and a bottle of champagne was thrust into my hands. Crowds gathered and photographers snapped pictures. It was quite surreal and more than slightly uncomfortable. Luckily, our paper had three other journalists on a team project who also won a Pulitzer that year, which helped spread the attention. Parties and TV interviews and all manner of nice attention ensued, plus a memorable trip to New York to pick up my prize. But looking back, one of the sweetest moments was when I — not the most demonstrative person in the world — had the opportunity to address our entire staff. I was able to tell them directly how proud I was to work with them at the Star Tribune. Without reporters and photographers and the assorted support staff, I'd have nothing to draw about. As they say, I only know what I read in the newspapers!

Following are some of the cartoons included in that year's contest entry. Others appear elsewhere in this book.

THE PULITZER PRIZE | 189

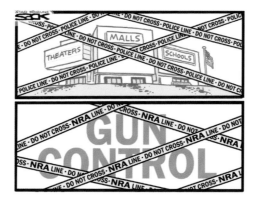

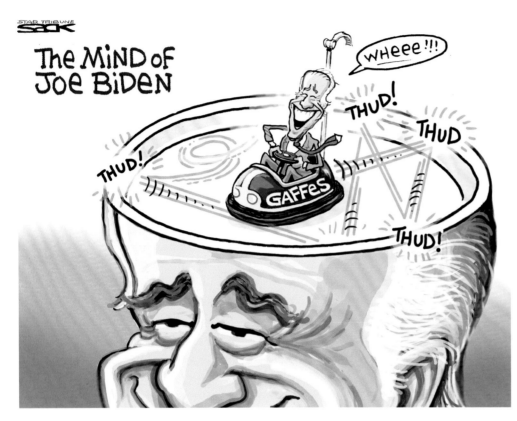

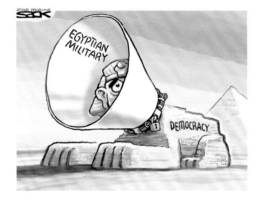

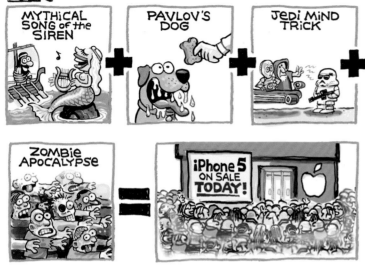

What other art do you do?

I've always enjoyed making other types of art. I should say "play" with other art, because all of my personal art projects inevitably have a similar goofy sensibility. I tend to go through phases — intensely focusing on a new medium for several years before abandoning it for something completely different. I've dabbled in ceramics, oil painting, three-dimensional digital art, animations, colored pencil, and sculpture (both kiln-fired ceramic and papier-mâché), wire, and even Minnesota State Fair seed art. I've designed art pillows, and tattoos. I'm sure that these side excursions affected my drawing style and approach to editorial cartooning in some way, but I can't put my finger on how, exactly. It's probably similar to a reporter writing the Great American Novel during lunch breaks — or an accountant dabbling in brain surgery on the weekends. Following are some examples.

Index

Epilogue

Finally, a special thank-you to the wonderful readers of the Star Tribune who have enjoyed/endured my scribblings for these many years. Whether you've given my work the high honor of display on your refrigerator, or have used it to line your pet's cage, it has been my pleasure indeed. Perhaps one day you'll find a collection of my next 8,000 cartoons in "The First and Only Book of Sack, Volume 2" — available in 2053 or thereabouts. Cheers.